The Compleat Child

The
Compleat Child

A Compendium of Etiquette,
Manners, and Poise
for Perfectly Marvelous
Girls and Boys

BY

LOIS WYSE

AND

JOAN JAVITS

ILLUSTRATED BY OUIDA

The World Publishing Company

Cleveland and New York

Published by The World Publishing Company
2231 West 110th Street, Cleveland, Ohio 44102
Published simultaneously in Canada by Nelson, Foster & Scott Ltd.

First Printing 1966

Contents

The Compleat Child

What are manners?
Well, first you ought to know what they are not.
They are not something you use once in a while.
Like dancing pumps.
They are not something you bring out especially for company.
Like thin mints.
Manners are something you have with you always.
Like freckles.
And if you have nice manners,
there are nice rewards.

Meeting People

Did you ever know any children
who forgot to introduce you to their friends?
Instead they ran and jumped and played
while you just stood there like a big lump.

Those children had unfriendly manners.

Children with friendly manners
introduce friends to friends:
"Charles Eclair, I'd like you to meet my friend, Harold Mocha-
Mousse."
They introduce parents to friends:
"Mother, this is Philippa Pheppermint."
They always put the name of the older person or of the woman
first.

Reward

They are most likely to meet pashas and potentates.

Inviting a Friend

Do you know a child
who slumps around the house kicking chairs and mumbling:
"I don't have anybody to play with"?

That child has distressing manners.
He also distresses the 18th-century armoire.

Children stressing manners say:
"Mother, may I have a friend come to visit today?"
They phone friends and say:
"Hello, Mrs. Robinson. May I please speak to Jack?"
And to Jack:
"Jack, this is Farnsworth. Will you come to my house to play today?"

Reward

Quick as you can say "Jack Robinson," there is a friend at your house.

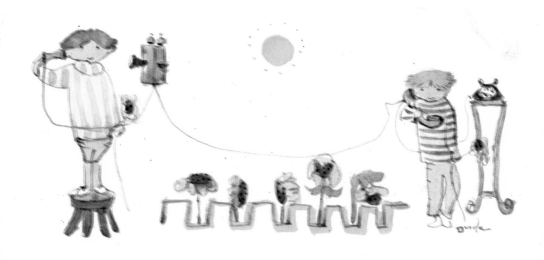

Just Talking

Did you ever notice that some children brag:
"Our estate has two swimming pools,
and yours has only one. Nah nah nah."
"Our cook soufflés higher than your cook."
"My father has A T & T preferred, and yours has A T & T
common."

These children have unboastable manners.

Children with boastable manners
invite friends to swim in their second pool,
soufflé their second cook,
and split shares of A T & T.

Reward

They get to walk up the steps of the Union Club two at a time.

Winning

Did you ever see a child at chess who says:
"Ha ha, queen check. I won. You're stupid"?

That child has unwinning manners.

Children with winning manners say:
"Maybe next time you will check my queen."

Reward

Good winners win good friends ... and the International Chess Championship.

Losing

Did you ever see a child who was losing
deflate the ball,
debean the bag,
or defeather the birdie?

That child had despicable manners.

Children with spicable manners
play the whole game to the whole end.
And smile.

Reward

They are elected captain of the Delray Polo Team.

Being Agreeable

Did you ever know a Nono?
A Nono is a child who always says:
"No. No."

A Nono has negative manners.

Children with positive manners say yes.

Reward

Do they get to do fun things like bone-fishing and skydiving?
Yesyes.

Going Home

Did anyone ever come to your house to rehearse chamber music
and just stay and stay
and stay and stay
and stay
until your mother had to ask if he were ever going home?

Manners played second fiddle with that child.

Children with first-fiddle manners think about going home
the very minute they arrive.
They tell the grown-up in charge when they must go home.
At going-home time they say:
"Goodbye,"
and they always say:
"Thank you, Mrs. Juilliard, I had a very nice time."
Of course, that is not what they say to Mrs. Guggenheim.

Reward

Children who go home allegro come back vivace.

Getting Up in the Morning

Did you ever hear children giggle upstairs
and galumpf downstairs
before the crack of dawn?

Those children had disturbing manners.

Children with undisturbing morning manners whisper (shhhhhh).
They play with crayons and a coloring book (shhhhhhh).
Then they dress themselves so quietly
you can hear a zipper zip (shhhhhhh).
Next they tiptoe downstairs (shhhhhhh)
and say loud and clear:
"GOOD MORNING."

Reward

They eat Eggs Benedict instead of Eggs Boiled.

Going to Bed at Night

Did you ever see a child at bedtime
demand a drink of Perrier water, an open window, a shut door,
an extra night light, another bedtime story, another drink of
Perrier, a trip to the w.c., a slightly less open door . . .
or just one more kiss?

That child had nightmarish manners.

Children with dreamy manners go straight to bed at bedtime.
Of course, they first
kiss Mama, Papa, and all the siblings,
curtsy to Cook and bow to Butler,
wash their faces, brush their teeth,
drink their Perrier,
say their prayers (may there never be a Perrier shortage),
and turn off the light . . . goodnight.

Reward

They have wide-screen, stereophonic dreams that win all the
prizes at the Cannes Festival.

Sleep-over Guests

Did you ever have a sleep-over guest
who came to your house complete with little suitcase
and said goodnight and got into bed
and then decided he didn't want to sleep over after all,
and your father had to get up, out of his nice warm bed
and drive the non-sleep-over back home?

That guest had two-poster manners.

Sleep-over guests with four-poster manners
arrive with pajamas and toothbrush and slippers, and
go to bed quickly and quietly.
In the morning they help make their bed and breakfast.
And a very good guest (sleep-over, eat-over, or any-over)
reciprocates.

Reward

Good sleep-overs find baba au rhum, spumoni, and eggnog
when they raid the refrigerator.
Bad sleep-overs find oranges, prune juice, and cauliflower.

[28]

At the Table

Did you ever see children
forget to use their napkins,
put their elbows on the table,
and talk with their mouths full of filet?

These children had unappetizing manners.

Children with appetizing manners
put napkins on their laps,
elbows at their sides,
and swallow (glunk) before they talk.

Reward
They are taken to State Dinners and coming-out parties.

Getting a Present

Did you ever go to a birthday party
and see the birthday child
grab presents out of other children's hands,
tear off the wrappings,
throw them on the floor,
and never even bother to say thank you?

That child was not gifted with manners.

A child with presentable manners
first finds the card.
He reads it, or has somebody big read it to him.
Then he opens the present neatly.
Then he thanks the person who gave it.
He doesn't just mumble thanksalot.
He says something special. For instance:
"Confucius' original ivory mah-jongg set! Oh thank you.
I can hardly wait to play."

Reward

Present givers become future receivers.

Writing a Thank-You Note

Did you ever know children
who received gifts
and never even wrote a teeny tiny note of thanks?

Thankless manners!

Children with thankful manners immediately send
teeny tiny notes that say:
"I am glad you remembered me."
Or:
"I love the present you sent me."
Or just plain:
"Thank you very much. Love."

Reward

They get very much. Love.

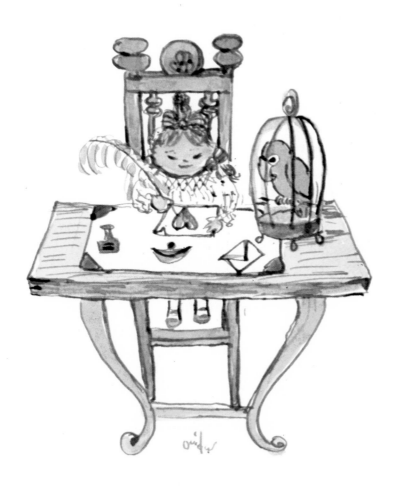

Writing a Letter

Did you ever rush to the mailbox
and wait and wait and wait—day after day after day
and not get a letter from someone who was supposed to send you
a letter?

The child who didn't write had disappointing manners.

Children with well-appointed manners answer letters promptly.
Their letters are full of newsy items . . .
They tell about Nana at the Veiled Prophet Ball
or Father's bid for the governorship.
They tell where they have been (Paris, Rome, or Gristede's)
and what they have done (the Louvre, the Colosseum, or peanut
butter).
And they always say something about the other person . . .
For instance:
"How are you and do you still have chicken pox?"

Reward

Their letters bring higher prices at Parke-Bernet.

In Car Pools

Do you notice the way
some children in car pools
turn the back seat into Yankee Stadium
and the front seat into Madison Square Garden?

These children have dangerous manners.

Children with safe manners
fasten their seat belts,
keep the shouting down,
and limit their hockey to the fields of Groton.

Reward
They get to sit beside the chauffeur in Carey car pools.

On the Playground

Did you ever see a boy on the playground
put his elbow in his best friend's ear to get to the top
of the jungle gym?
Did you ever see a girl on the playground
knock down three teachers to get to the swings?

Those children had outrageous manners.

Children with rageous manners
climb while others catch,
see while others saw,
and wait in line to glide, slide, ride, and hide.

Reward
Their Ace Bandages last a long time.

In a Restaurant

Did you ever see children in restaurants
pound on the table,
spill things on purpose,
blow straws across the room,
and tip back in their chairs
so that waiters carrying bouillabaisse almost fell over them?

Those children had zero manners.

Children with "21" manners
order quickly and quietly with their parents' help.
They try to eat neat.

Reward
They get to order profiteroles.

At the Cinema

Did you ever see children at the cinema
squirm, wiggle, and run up and down the aisles
to buy popcorn,
get a drink,
or go to the bathroom
and then talkety-talk-talk all through the picture?

Those children had impossible manners.

Children with possible manners
sit in their seats and watch the film.
Quietly.

Reward

They never miss a Fellini.

At Dancing Class

Did you ever know girls in dancing class
who always came late
and forgot their leotards or tap shoes or entrechat?

Those children were not on their toes.

Children with graceful manners come to dancing class
(or any place) a little early
so they won't be late.
They organize their dancing things
and put them in a little suitcase or a little something
so no one will have to wait while one child hunts for one hairband.
And between lessons
they practice so they won't forget what they've learned.

Reward

They get to wear sequined tutus in *Swan Lake*.

In the Toy Department

Did you ever see children in the toy department
poke their fingers through the cellophane packages and say:
"I want this. I want that. I want I want I want"?

Those children had unwanted manners.

Children with wanted manners never poke packages or parents.
They never fold their hands behind their backs.
And they never say, "I want," although they want, too.

Reward

Their parents want to.

At a Hotel

Have you ever seen children at a hotel
do handstands in the lobby,
play buzz-and-hide with the elevators,
and throw inkwells out the window?

Those children had boarding-house manners.

Children with Grand Hotel manners
walk sedately through lobbies,
ride sedately on lifts,
and leave inkwells sedately alone.

Reward

They get to order croissants from Room Service.

At the Zoo

Have you ever stood in front of a sign that says:
DO NOT FEED OR ANNOY THE ANIMALS
while annoying children fed the animals?
Have you ever stood in front of the sign that says:
NO LITTERING
with a litter of littering children?

Beastly manners!

Children with good manners
do not have to be put on a leash to go to the zoo.

Reward
They are invited on African safaris.

In the House of God

Did you ever go to church (or temple)
and see some children squirming, talking, giggling, and
playing tic-tac-toe in their hymnals?

Those children had ungodly manners.

Children with angelic manners
look at the pretty colored-glass windows.
They listen to the music.
They try to sit when everyone sits, stand when everyone stands,
kneel when everyone kneels, bow heads when everyone bows.
They speak with reverence in the House of God.

Reward

God listens.

At the Dentist

Do you know a child who
stamps, hoots, and bangs his dear little head on the floor
every time his mother says:
"You must go to see the dentist"?

He has unpolished manners.

Children with polished manners
hop in the elevator chair and ride up and down,
open very wide when the dentist tells them to,
let the dentist fix their bicuspids and peppermint-polish their
molars,
and always smile when they come in
and smile when they go out.

Reward

They have bicuspids and molars to smile with.

On the Bus

Did you ever ride on a bus
and see children scramble into the seats
while grown-ups were standing?
And did you ever see children stand on the seats,
so ladies in white dresses
who sat on the seats afterward
had black-and-white dresses
when they got off the bus?

Manners like these should move to the rear.

Children with up-front manners give their seats to
old ladies, old men, young ladies, young men, and
little girls (particularly if they are little boys).

Reward

When they are old and tired and thirty, well-mannered children
will give them their seats.

In a Plane

Have you ever flown in an airplane
and watched children running up and down the aisle whining,
"When will we get there?"

Those children had turbulent manners.

Children with smooth manners prepare for smooth plane rides.
If the flight is to be a long one,
they take along Autobridge and Double-Crostics.

Reward

They think they get there faster.

On a Boat

Did you ever go sailing with children
who simply would not pay attention,
and so they
downed when they should have upped,
upped when they should have downed,
and bounced around so much that their poor daddies
got bopped with the boom?

They had unworthy manners.

Children with seaworthy manners wear life preservers always,
and they obey instructions.
Quickly.
They do not bounce around when their daddies are
raising the sail, lowering the sail,
or reading the book to find out what to do next.

Reward

They get a turn at the tiller, and they never get dunked in the
drink.

On Bicycles

Have you ever seen children
ride their bicycles (or tricycles)
in the middle of the street,
or have you seen them zoom down the sidewalk lickety-split,
practically knocking people on their left ear?

Those children had free-wheeling manners.

Children with well-balanced manners
ride bikes on the sidewalk only.
They ring the bells on their bikes,
and they are very careful not to run over
people,
pets, and
parents.
They remember to bring their bicycles in out of the rain,
and they never leave a bike in the driveway.

Reward

They never have battered bikes or dented daddies.

On the Telephone

Did you ever hear a child speaking on the telephone who said:
"Who is this?" or
"What do you want?" or
"TELEPHONE!"

That child had unspeakable manners.

Children with speakable manners answer the telephone by saying:
"Fitzenheimer residence, Francesca speaking."
Instead of screaming, they run to fetch their fathers.
They never talk, tear, or tug at mothers (or anyone) talking on the phone.

Reward

Francesca Fitzenheimers get to place conference calls on credit cards.

With Television

Do you know a child
who thinks the TV set belongs to him and no one else
and turns his programs on so loud
that his poor mother has to hold her hands over her ears,
and if anyone switches channels,
he falls to the floor and turns magenta?

That child has unchanneled manners.

Children with channeled manners let other people in the family
choose programs too.

Reward

They get to watch the "Late Late Movie."

Reading a Book

Did you ever see children with books
who practiced op art in the margins
and dropped globs of pâté on the covers
and broke the bindings and (sob)
tore the pages out?

Those children had unprintable manners.

Children with printable manners
make sure their hands are clean before they handle books.
They never open the pages so wide that the bindings break.
They are careful not to tear even one page a wee bit.
They use bookmarks to find their place.
They treat books like good friends.

Reward

They get complete and unabridged sets of first-
edition William Shakespeare for their birthdays.

Swimming

Did you ever go to a swimming pool or beach and see children
push other children into the water,
splash grown-ups,
duck friends, and
kick sand?

Their manners were all wet.

Children with dry manners
stay at the children's end of the pool
(or where there is adult supervision).
They never splash or duck anybody...
especially anybody's mother...
especially their own mothers who have just had their hair done.

Reward

They get accepted at the best clubs.

Buying Clothes

Did you ever see a mother
shop with a child,
and the child
fidget-ed, squidget-ed, fussed, and said,
"I HATE THAT!"

That child had unfit manners.

Children with fit manners
never make faces at something they see on a counter or on a
hanger.
They try it on, if their mothers think they should.
And they bend and reach and stretch in the new whatever-it-is
so their mothers can see if whatever-it-is fits properly,
and they won't outgrow it on the way home.
Children with fit manners never have fits when the fitter fits.

Reward

They never get stuck with pins at a Mainbocher fitting.

When Parents Have Parties

Did you ever know a child who
whined,
screamed,
called, "Daddy,"
came downstairs,
peeked around doors,
took all the hors d'oeuvres off the trays,
and played "Chopsticks" on the piano as loud as he could
when his parents had a party?

That child did not have party manners.

Children with party manners
stay in bed once they are put in bed.

Reward

They are served champagne ginger ale in their rooms.

On Parents' Birthdays and Wedding Anniversaries

Did you ever hear a child say:
"What am I getting What am I getting What am I getting?"
and never say (even to himself):
"What can I give What can I give What can I give?"

That child had unthinkable manners.

Children with thinkable manners think
their parents would like to be remembered too,
on birthdays and anniversaries and Christmas and
Valentine's Day and Mother's Day and Father's Day.
And even if children don't have two pennies,
they know they can give a present . . .
because the best present is the gift of one's self.
A child can write a sonnet, or make a collage,
or pick a bouquet, or bake petits fours,
or something, for goodness' sake.

Reward

The very nice feeling of being good for goodness' sake.

With Brothers and Sisters

Did you ever see
brothers and sisters
shout,
stamp,
pull each other's hair,
and call one another "Stupid Head"?

Those children had warlike manners.

Brothers and sisters with peaceful manners
share toys, books, parents, and chores.
And . . . sometimes . . .
without anyone ever asking,
they do each other a favor.

Reward

Brother is introduced to every link of the Daisy Chain, and
Sister marries the president of Brother's class at Princeton.

With Chambermaids,

COOKS, GOVERNESSES, CHAUFFEURS, GARDENERS, FOOTMEN . . . OH YES, AND THE CLEANING WOMAN TOO

Some children are very nasty to the help at home.
They refer to "my maid" and stamp their feet and say:
"I WON'T!"
or bark orders:
"Make my bed." "I want my lunch right now."
"Take me out." "Drive me." "Clean my room."

These children have no command of manners.

Children with a command of manners do not command.
They ask. Nicely.
"Would you please serve the escargots for dinner tonight?"
"Would you please drive me to the Ball tonight?"
And they always say: "Thank you."

Reward

They get to lick bowls of marzipan and push floor polishers,
and they are put on the Tiffany mailing list.

With Teachers

Do you know any children
who talk when the teacher is talking
and talk during show and tell
and talk during rest period
and talk talk talk talk talk,
except when the teacher asks them to talk?
Then they have nothing to say.

Detestable!

Children with testable manners
are very quiet
unless the teacher asks them to speak.
They are very quiet
because they are listening and learning.

Reward
They become Phi Beta Kappas at a very early age.

With Pets

WITH DOGS, CATS, RABBITS, BIRDS, FISH, GUINEA PIGS,
HAMSTERS, FROGS, LADYBUGS, OR WHAT-HAVE-YOUS

Did you ever know children who
needled, wheedled, begged, teased, and sobbed
to get a pet?
And the first day they
fed it, petted it, cleaned it, played with it,
and loved it?
And the second day they starved it?

Those children had inhuman manners.

Children with human manners
pet pets every day
and make sure their pets always have water and a clean place to
sleep.

Reward

They win all the blue ribbons at the Horse Show at Madison
Square Garden. Unless, of course, they have hamsters.

Giving a Party

Did you ever go to a birthday buffet or Bal Masque
where the host said:
"Hellohowareyoutakeyourcoatoff"
and then ran off to pin tails on donkeys
with children you didn't even know?

That host had uninviting manners.

Hosts (and hostesses) with inviting manners offer
a piece of cake (with a sugar rosette),
a pink balloon,
a donkey's tail,
and a jolly good time.

Reward

The Duchess speaks well of them in her memoirs.

In the Supermarket

Isn't it just awful the way some children supermarket?
They pull out the very bottom can of mock turtle soup and—
CRASH.
They use carts like scooters, skid around corners, and—
CRASH.
They climb on the moving checkout counter and—
CRASH.

Crashing bad manners!

Children with super manners
take nothing from shelves.
They sit nicely in the basket (if they still fit)
or walk nicely next to the basket (if they don't fit)
or wait nicely while their mothers check out.

Reward

Huntington Hartford, his heirs, and assigns are pleased.

At the Library

Have you ever been reading or studying
in the children's room while
some bibliophiles babbled, others bobbled,
and a few chased each other around the bookshelves
and threw paper airplanes at the librarian?

Those children had unprintable manners.

Children with printable manners
Shhhhhhh in the library,
bring their library cards,
take very good care of the books they borrow,
and never have to pay fines.

Reward

They can tell Santa Claus from Santayana.

At Daddy's Office

Did you ever know any children who sat at their daddies' desks,
buzzed all the buzzers,
de-inked all the pens,
tickered with the tape,
and made three Girls Friday plus one Girl Wednesday quit on
the spot?

Bullish manners!

Children with bearable manners
never touch
ticker tapes,
typewriters,
telephones,
comptometers,
postage meters, or
adding machines.

Reward

They get to work the soft-drink machine.

With Sitters

Once upon a time there was a little child
who shouted and shrieked the very minute his parents left the
house.
He would not (scream scream) go to bed on time.
He would not (stamp stamp) brush his teeth.
He would throw all his toys up in the air
and jump on his bed until the springs sprung.

Such insidious manners!

Children with sidious manners
get ready for bed on time.
They brush their teeth and comb their hair, and
sometimes they even wash their faces.

Reward

Royal sitters will stand for them.

At the Museum

Did you ever study Pithecanthropus erectus at the Natural History
Museum
or Picasso at the Museum of Art
or planets at the Planetarium
while children
chewed peanuts, juggled popcorn,
pushed, punched,
and got lost?

Those children were exhibitionists.

Children with manners worth exhibiting
stay with their group,
listen to the lecturer,
and never litter or loiter.

Reward

They become eligible for the
Nobel Prize for Scientific and Artistic Behavior.

Manners for the Audience

At Carnegie Hall
did you ever sit behind a child
who swayed back and forth like a string section
or in front of a child
who beat your seat like a rhythm section
or beside a child
who made more noise than a brass section?

Such disconcerting manners.

Children with manners worth applauding
do not put on a performance in the audience.
They start by sitting still.
They end by still sitting.

Reward

Critics give them unanimous raves.

At the Doctor's

Did you ever sit in the waiting room and hear a child shriek,
"I DON'T WANT A TRIPLE BOOSTER"?
And then did you ever hear a child scream
while he got a triple booster?
And then did you ever see a doctor and nurse
after they gave a triple booster?

Unindoctrinated manners!

Children doctrinated in manners
grit their teeth and are kind to the dear doctor
who gives a lot more shots than they take.

Reward

Patient patients stay healthy, for goodness' Salk.

Asking Questions

Did you ever know a child who said loud and clear:
"Why doesn't that man have any hair on his head?"
"Why is that lady bigger than that man?"
or just plain
"Who is that?"

That child had questionable manners.

Children with unquestionably good manners
look now and ask later.

Reward

They get taken to State Dinners and Annual Meetings.

When Someone Is Ill

Did you know that
when Samantha's great-aunt was ill,
some children came to visit Samantha
and played blindman's buff in the upstairs hall
and slid down the bannister four at a time
and absolutely raised the roof?

Undoubtedly you do not know those ill-mannered children.

Well-mannered children
are especially considerate of those who are ill.
They make and send pretty little get-well cards
or pick flowers
or do Something Thoughtful . . .
like inviting the children of somebody ill to play at *their* houses.

Reward

People never get sick of children with good manners.

Celebrating Christmas

There has never been a naughty child on December 24 at 7 P.M.
But, oh my, did you ever see a child on December 26
sitting on a pile of toys with a rocket in one hand
and the keys to a new Thunderbird in the other
shouting, "You can't make me"?

Children like that are not celebrated for their manners.

Children with festive manners
thank their parents for cleaning the chimney and
letting Santa come through with the presents.
They take turns opening gifts so everyone can see
and mothers can keep track of who got what.
Then they find a new place for the new toys
and clean up the old mess.

Reward

Santa Claus believes in them.

Celebrating Halloween

Did you ever know a child who put on a devil's mask
and then acted like a real devil?

That child had frightful manners.

Children with UNICEF manners
say "thank you" for treats
and "no thank you" to tricks.

Reward

The goblins don't get them . . . and neither do the
juvenile authorities.

With Grandparents, Indulgent Aunts, Rich Uncles, and Other Relatives

Did you ever know any children
who had not seen their grandparents for six years and twelve days
and, when their grandparents came to visit,
looked up from their Tinker Toys
(which their grandparents had sent them for Christmas)
just long enough to say,
"What did you bring me?"

Those children had relatively no manners.

Well-mannered children rise and rush to kiss
grandmamas, grandpapas,
and all other grand relations.
They say:
"I love you."
"I have missed you."
"I'm so glad you came to see me."

Reward

Their grandparents open charge accounts at F. A. O. Schwarz.

Just for Girls

Did you ever see girls who stumbled and mumbled
when they were introduced to people?
Or did you ever know a girl
who came to tea
and sat on her chin with her left leg wrapped around the lamp?

Those girls had unladylike manners.

Ladies curtsy when they are introduced and say,
"How do you do?"
And at teatime . . . or any time . . .
you will find them sitting pretty:
knees together, ankles crossed.
Young ladies let older ladies (and gentlemen too)
walk through doors ahead of them.
After being introduced, young ladies always say,
"It was very nice meeting you."

Reward

Little ladies grow up to be big ladies.

Just for Boys

Do you know boys who leapfrog
over hydrants, prams, and little old ladies
just so they can be first through the door?

These boys have ungentlemanly manners.

Gentlemen rise when a lady enters the room.
They remove their hats when entering buildings or elevators.
They shake hands when introduced, and say,
"How do you do?" and always address older gentlemen as "Sir."
They pull out dining chairs and help seat ladies at the table.
They open and hold doors for all grown-ups and all girls.

Reward

Wherever they go, doors are opened for them,
because gentlemen are welcome anywhere in the world.

Something for Everybody

Have you ever had a grown-up say to you,
"Charles, fetch the *Times* financial section," or
"I remember you when you were this big," or
"Do you look like your mother or your father?" or
"What grade are you in now?"

Those grown-ups had infantile manners.

Grown-ups with adult manners
talk to children as if children were real live people.
They ask if you have been to the zoo lately
and tell you about the new platypus there.
Or they ask you something sensible, for instance,
"Are you going to Europe this summer?"

Reward

Grown-ups with good manners have many friends,
and some of their best friends are children.

The Compleat Glossary

Meeting People

PASHA: Rhymes with cash-a, which is what a pasha has-a.

POTENTATE: The supreme absolute ruler, also known as daddy and/or mommy.

Inviting a Friend

ARMOIRE: An old chest made fashionable by people who live in small apartments and have absolutely no closet space.

Just Talking

A T & T: American Telephone & Telegraph. This is to fathers what Santa Claus is to children.

Going Home

ALLEGRO: The speed at which a child walks home from school.

VIVACE: The speed at which a child walks home from school if it is his birthday and there is a very big present waiting for him and he knows it.

Getting Up in the Morning

EGGS BENEDICT: An English muffin topped with a slice of ham topped with a poached egg topped with hollandaise topped with truffles. And, in the egg family, nothing tops this.

Going to Bed at Night

PERRIER WATER: Faucet water in a bottle that is drunk when one does not trust faucet water in a faucet.

Sleep-over Guests

BABA AU RHUM: Drunken sponge cake.

SPUMONI: Italian ices, known also as gelati, known also as green, white, and brown ice cream with fruit.

EGGNOG: A drink made of milk and eggs and nutmeg, usually served at Christmas time and so good you'll wonder why you don't like milk and eggs more than you do.

At the Table

FILET: What's left of fish or meat when the bones are removed.

STATE DINNERS: Fancy government dinners at which officials work themselves into a real state.

Getting a Present

CONFUCIUS: A very wise and ancient Chinese gentleman who said very wise and ancient things (e.g., "Those who err on the side of strictness are few indeed").

Writing a Letter

VEILED PROPHET BALL: It's New Orleans' Mardi Gras and New York's Cotillion, and it happens in St. Louis.

GRISTEDE'S: The rich lady's A & P.

PARKE-BERNET: An art museum where everything is for sale.

In Car Pools

YANKEE STADIUM: An empty field where grown men play baseball.

MADISON SQUARE GARDEN: An indoor Yankee Stadium where (despite the name) nothing blooms except prizefighters, show dogs, show horses, and an occasional speechmaker.

GROTON: Rhymes with rotten, which Groton isn't. What Groton *is* is a very fine preparatory school for very fine young gentlemen.

CAREY CAR POOLS: Carey is a car-rental agency where one can hire Cadillacs and chauffeurs. People who ride in Carey car pools are usually not as rich as they feel.

On the Playground

ACE BANDAGE: A heavy gauze used to bind sore muscles; the Purple Heart of athletics.

In a Restaurant

BOUILLABAISSE: A fish soup that is as difficult to make as it is to pronounce.

21: A terrific restaurant in New York City for people over 21 (able to pay over $21 for lunch).

PROFITEROLE: An éclair with chocolate-covered calories.

At the Cinema

FELLINI: The James Joyce of film producers.

At Dancing Class

LEOTARDS: Stretch tights. If men wear them, they are called long underwear.

ENTRECHAT: What Nureyev does so well.

TUTU: What Margot Fonteyn wears so well.

SWAN LAKE: What Tchaikovsky wrote so well that Nureyev and Fonteyn perform so well.

At a Hotel

CROISSANTS: Pronounced cruh-wah-sahn. It is pronounced even better with jam, because a croissant is a flaky roll shaped like a new moon.

ROOM SERVICE: What hotels have instead of mothers.

At the Zoo

AFRICAN SAFARIS: Big Game for Big People played on a Big Continent.

At the Dentist

BICUSPIDS: Some teeth.

MOLARS: Some more teeth.

In a Plane

AUTOBRIDGE: The only bridge game in which you can trump your partner's ace with impunity.

DOUBLE-CROSTICS: A crossword puzzle no one can do.

On a Boat

TILLER: The steering stick on a boat.

BOOM: The other stick on a boat.

On the Telephone

CONFERENCE CALLS: Eight people on one telephone line discussing the weather in East Orange.

CREDIT CARDS: What fathers use instead of money.

With Television

MAGENTA: A reddish-purple color, which practically nothing is.

Reading a Book

OP ART: This year's pop art.

PÂTÉ: Gooseliver that is ground and chopped and seasoned so well it deserves a better name than gooseliver.

Buying Clothes

MAINBOCHER: The dressmaker of the world's most elegant women; despite his elegant French name and elegant French atelier, he is an American.

On Parents' Birthdays and Wedding Anniversaries

SONNET: Three quatrains and a couplet written in iambic pentameter. Millions of people write bad sonnets, but two people write good sonnets: William Shakespeare and Elizabeth Barrett Browning.

COLLAGE: Bits and pieces of this and that all thrown together. In cooking it is called hash.

PETITS FOURS: Little cakes that take a long time to make and no time to eat.

With Brothers and Sisters

DAISY CHAIN: The flower of the Ivy League that blooms at Vassar College.

PRINCETON: A good school rarely attended by boys from Groton only because it is not Harvard.

With Chambermaids, etc.

ESCARGOTS: A dish served in French restaurants and so named in order that people who have never eaten snails and never would will.

MARZIPAN: A paste of nuts that is shaped like fruit and tastes like candy.

TIFFANY: A very expensive toy store for grown-ups.

With Teachers

PHI BETA KAPPA: A very smart club. Literally.

Giving a Party

BAL MASQUE: An enormous party where grown-ups play dress-up.

MEMOIRS: What famous people write when they stop doing things and think about what they did.

In the Supermarket

HUNTINGTON HARTFORD: A man who founded a museum in New York and founded a hotel on an island all because his ancestors founded A & P.

At the Library

BIBLIOPHILES: Human bookworms.

SANTAYANA: A philosopher who bears absolutely no resemblance to Santa Claus or any other writer.

At Daddy's Office

GIRL FRIDAY: A girl who is willing to work on Sunday; other girls who work are secretaries.

At the Museum

PITHECANTHROPUS ERECTUS: What you would have been if you had been born in —— B.C.

PICASSO: The painter who influenced art as much as Pithecanthropus erectus influenced man.

NOBEL PRIZE: An award given by the government of Sweden to people who are not always recognized by their own governments.

At the Doctor's

TRIPLE BOOSTER: A doctor's three-for-one sale.

FOR GOODNESS' SALK: Dr. Jonas Salk developed the vaccine to prevent infantile paralysis. Thank goodness.

Asking Questions

ANNUAL MEETINGS: The once-a-year day when corporations tell stockholders what they will do with their money, and stockholders tell corporations what they can do with their corporations.

Celebrating Halloween

UNICEF: Collecting funds for UNICEF keeps Halloween from being such a hollow day.

With Grandparents, etc.

F. A. O. SCHWARZ: A store where children are often taken to select the Christmas toys their parents will buy at Macy's.

Just for Girls

LADY: A woman with manners, etiquette, and poise.

Just for Boys

GENTLEMAN: A man with manners, etiquette, and poise.

Something for Everybody

FINANCIAL SECTION: The part of the paper that fathers read, mothers ignore, and dogs get spanked with.

PLATYPUS: A very difficult animal to describe. Why don't you go to the zoo and see one for yourself?

Yellow Umbrella Books are published by Capstone Press
151 Good Counsel Drive, P.O. Box 669, Mankato, Minnesota 56002
http://www.capstone-press.com

Library of Congress Cataloging-in-Publication Data
Catala, Ellen.
Ways we communicate / by Ellen Catala.
p. cm.
Includes Index.
Summary: Introduces what communication is and some of the different ways
in which people communicate with one another.
ISBN 0-7368-2029-9 (alk. paper)
1. Communication–Juvenile literature. [1. Communication.] I. Title.
P91.2.C34 2003
302.2–dc21
2003000927

Editorial Credits
Mary Lindeen, Editorial Director; Jennifer Van Voorst, Editor; Wanda Winch, Photo Researcher

Photo Credits
Cover: Tomi/PhotoLink/PhotoDisc; Title Page: Ryan McVay/PhotoDisc; Page 2: Comstock;
Page 3: Larry Mulvehill/Corbis; Page 4: Rob Van Petten/DigitalVision; Page 5: Doug
Menuez/PhotoDisc; Page 6: Steve Mason/PhotoDisc; Page 7: Creatas; Page 8: D. Berry/
PhotoLink/PhotoDisc; Page 9: Nicole Sutton/Life File/PhotoLink/PhotoDisc; Page 10: Stockbyte;
Page 11: Creative Concept/Index Stock; Page 12: Gaye Hilsenrath/Index Stock; Page 13: Defense
Visual Information Center; Page 14: Image Farm; Page 15: Image Farm; Page 16: BananaStock

Ways We Communicate

By Ellen Catala

Consultant: Mark J. Braun, Ph.D., Associate Dean of the College and
Associate Professor of Communication Studies,
Gustavus Adolphus College

Yellow Umbrella Books
an imprint of Capstone Press
Mankato, Minnesota

To communicate means to share ideas.

People do this in different ways.

Sometimes people get together and talk.

Getting together is a way to communicate.

Sometimes people talk on the phone.

Talking is a way
to communicate.

Sometimes people write letters.

Writing letters is a way to communicate.

Sometimes people write lists or notes.

Writing lists or notes is a way to communicate.

Sometimes people use hand signals.

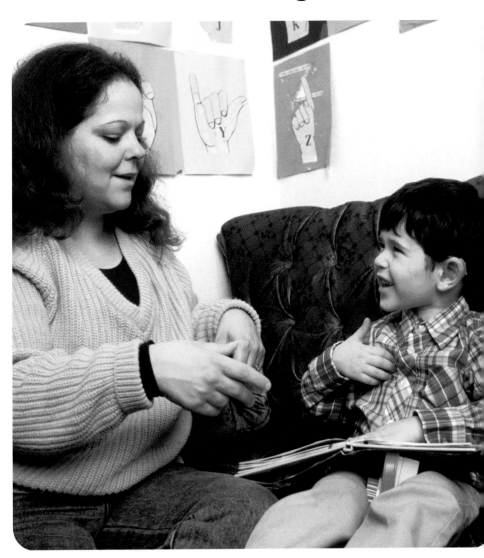

Using hand signals is a way to communicate.

Sometimes people use signs.

Using signs is a way to communicate.

Sometimes people just let their faces say it all!

Words to Know/Index

Word Count: 96
Early-Intervention Level: 6